PREHISTORIC SEA REPTILES

DINO-SORTED!

CLASSIFY THE FEATURES OF PREHISTORIC CREATURES

SONYA NEWLAND

Gareth Stevens PUBLISHING

Please visit our website, www.garethstevens.com. For a free color catalog of all our high-quality books, call toll free 1-800-542-2595 or fax 1-877-542-2596.

Cataloging-in-Publication Data
Names: Newland, Sonya.
Title: Prehistoric sea reptiles / Sonya Newland.
Description: Buffalo, NY : Gareth Stevens Publishing, 2026. | Series: Dino-sorted! | Includes glossary and index.
Identifiers: ISBN 9781482473698 (pbk.) | ISBN 9781482473704 (library bound) | ISBN 9781482473711 (ebook)
Subjects: LCSH: Marine reptiles, Fossil--Juvenile literature. | Marine reptiles, Fossil--Classification--Juvenile literature.
Classification: LCC QE861.N483 2026 | DDC 567.937--dc23

Published in 2026 by
Gareth Stevens Publishing
2544 Clinton St.
Buffalo, NY 14224

First published in Great Britain in 2021 by
The Watts Publishing Group

Credits
Editor: Sonya Newland
Designer: Clare Nicholas

The publisher would like to thank the following for permission to reproduce their pictures:

Alamy: Stocktrek Images, Inc. 7b, 8–9, 23b, 27t, 28–29, Universal Images Group North America LLC/DeAgostini 11t; Getty Images: Nobumichi Tamura/Stocktrek Images 10–11; Shutterstock: Konstantin G cover, 24–25, Catmando 4l, 5, 6–7, 11b, 13, 15b, Valentyna Chukhlyebova 4r, Lapis 2380 7t, Alizada Studios 9, Warpaint 12–13, 19t, 22, 26–27, Daniel Eskridge 14, 21, 25, Noiel 15t, Martin Weber 16–17, Michael Rosskothen 17, SciePro 18, Lefteris Papaulakis 19b, Herschel Hoffmeyer 20–21, Danny Ye23t, Ibe van Oort 27b, Esteban de Armas 29.

All design elements from Shutterstock.

Printed in the United States of America

CPSIA compliance information: Batch #CSGS26: For further information contact Gareth Stevens at 1-800-542-2595.

PRONUNCIATION GUIDE

Elasmosaurus (el-LAZ-mo-SORE-us)
Eurhinosaurus (yoo-rye-no-SORE-us)
Henodus (HEN-oh-dus)
Ichthyosaurus (ick-thee-oh-SORE-us)
Keichousaurus (kay-chow-SORE-us)
Kronosaurus (krow-no-SORE-us)
Lariosaurus (la-ree-oh-SORE-us)
Liopleurodon (lie-oh-PLOOR-oh-don)
Mosasaurus (moe-za-SORE-us)
Muraenosaurus (mu-RAY-no-SORE-us)
Nothosaurus (no-foe-SORE-us)
Paraplacodus (pah-ra-PLAK-o-dus)
Peloneustes (pel-oh-NEW-steez)
Placodus (PLAK-o-dus)
Platecarpus (plat-e-CAR-pus)
Plesiosaurus (pleh-see-oh-SORE-us)
Prognathodon (pro-NAYF-o-don)
Shastasaurus (shas-ta-SORE-us)
Shonisaurus (sho-nee-SORE-us)
Simolestes (si-mo-LES-teez)
Styxosaurus (sticks-oh-SORE-us)
Tylosaurus (tie-lo-SORE-us)

CONTENTS

MEET THE

THE PREHISTORIC SEAS WERE TEEMING WITH LIFE. JUST AS DINOSAURS RULED THE LAND, THE OCEANS WERE RULED BY HUGE SWIMMING REPTILES. THEY CAN BE SORTED INTO GROUPS ACCORDING TO THEIR FEATURES.

The nothosaurs and the ichthyosaurs emerged in the Early to Mid Triassic Period, just as the dinosaurs were settling into life on land. Later they were joined by other ocean hunters: plesiosaurs, pliosaurs, and mosasaurs. Although these groups were all quite different from each other, they did share some features. For example, they had streamlined shapes and flippers to help them swim at speed.

EARLY TRIASSIC SEA REPTILES	MID TRIASSIC SEA REPTILES	LATE TRIASSIC SEA REPTILES
Placodus	*Lariosaurus*	*Henodus*
	Keichousaurus	*Ichthyosaurus*
	Nothosaurus	*Shonisaurus*
	Paraplacodus	
	Shastasaurus	

TRIASSIC PERIOD

(252 to 201 million years ago)

REPTILES OF THE SEA

Kronosaurus

EARLY JURASSIC SEA REPTILES

Eurhinosaurus
Plesiosaurus

MID JURASSIC SEA REPTILES

Liopleurodon
Muraenosaurus
Peloneustes
Simolestes

JURASSIC PERIOD
(201 to 145 million years ago)

CRETACEOUS SEA REPTILES

Elasmosaurus
Kronosaurus
Mosasaurus
Platecarpus
Prognathodon
Styxosaurus
Tylosaurus

CRETACEOUS PERIOD
(145 to 66 million years ago)

Many of these giant sea reptiles survived until the end of the Late Cretaceous Period. At that time, about 66 million years ago, they were wiped out in a mass extinction event. Scientists believe that a huge asteroid came crashing into Earth in the area that is now Mexico. The collision created so much gas and dust that it changed Earth's climate dramatically. Many creatures, on land and in the sea, could not survive.

TRIASSIC PLACODONTS

AROUND THE TIME THE GIANT SEA REPTILES WERE EMERGING, THE OCEANS WERE ALSO HOME TO A GROUP OF SMALLER REPTILES CALLED PLACODONTS. THESE CREATURES LIVED ONLY DURING THE TRIASSIC PERIOD—THEY HAD ALL DIED OUT BY ABOUT 201 MILLION YEARS AGO.

Placodus used its forward-leaning front teeth to catch shellfish. It then used flat teeth at the back of its mouth to crush the seafood.

Placodonts first appeared in the Early Triassic Period. The earliest species, such as *Placodus* and *Paraplacodus*, looked like large lizards with big, barrel-shaped bodies. These reptiles could grow up to 6.5 feet (2 m) long.

By the Mid Triassic Period, sharks and larger carnivorous reptiles, such as ichthyosaurs and nothosaurs, arrived in the oceans. Placodonts began to develop bony plates on their backs to defend themselves from predators. These "shells" were large enough to protect their body and most of their limbs from the jaws of any ocean hunter!

By the Late Triassic Period, many placodonts had developed a complete bony shell on their backs, similar to the sea turtles that were evolving at the same time. This is a giant Cretaceous turtle called *Protostega*.

Reptiles don't have gills like fish. They have lungs and breathe air. This meant that placodonts–and other sea reptiles–could not breathe underwater and had to hold their breath when diving for food. As the placodonts evolved, they got heavier. This extra weight probably helped them to reach the bottom of the sea, where shellfish live.

Placodonts probably spent a lot of time on shore, going into the water to hunt.

SORTED:

HENODUS

THE LATE TRIASSIC *HENODUS* LOOKED A BIT LIKE A LARGE, FLAT TURTLE. IT IS THE ONLY PLACODONT THAT MAY HAVE LIVED IN FRESHWATER LAGOONS RATHER THAN IN THE OPEN SEA.

QUICK FACTS

PERIOD:
Late Triassic

LIVED IN:
Europe

LENGTH:
3.3 feet (1 m)

WEIGHT:
100 pounds (45 kg)

SNOUT

Henodus's snout looked a bit like a beak. The blunt end of the snout gave the placodont a square, boxy-looking head! At the back of the snout were two upper teeth that *Henodus* used for crushing its shellfish prey.

UNUSUAL TEETH

Henodus means "turtle-faced single tooth." It gets its name from the single tooth it had on each side of its mouth. Along its jaw were denticles–a row of thin, tooth-like structures. These suggest that *Henodus* ate using a kind of filter system, like some whales.

SHELL

The underside of the shell was made up of several flat bones that were fused to the spine. The top of the shell, called the carapace, was slightly curved, although it was flatter than the shells of modern turtles.

DINOMIGHTY!

Henodus's shell was twice as wide as it was long–stretching out wider than the placodont's feet, like armored wings!

LEGS AND FEET

Henodus had paddle-like legs and feet, which were good for moving through water. Its legs would have been quite weak on land, which made walking difficult. This reptile probably came to shore to rest and breed, but it would not have traveled far inland.

LONG-TAILED NOTHOSAURS

THE NOTHOSAURS WERE AMONG THE EARLIEST LARGE SEA-LIVING REPTILES. THEY EVOLVED FROM LAND ANIMALS AND WERE SEMI-AQUATIC, WHICH MEANS THEY SPENT SOME OF THEIR TIME IN THE SEA AND SOME ON LAND.

In the water, many nothosaurs probably looked a bit like crocodiles, although some had smaller heads. They had long, flat tails and short legs. They swam by moving their body and tail from side to side.

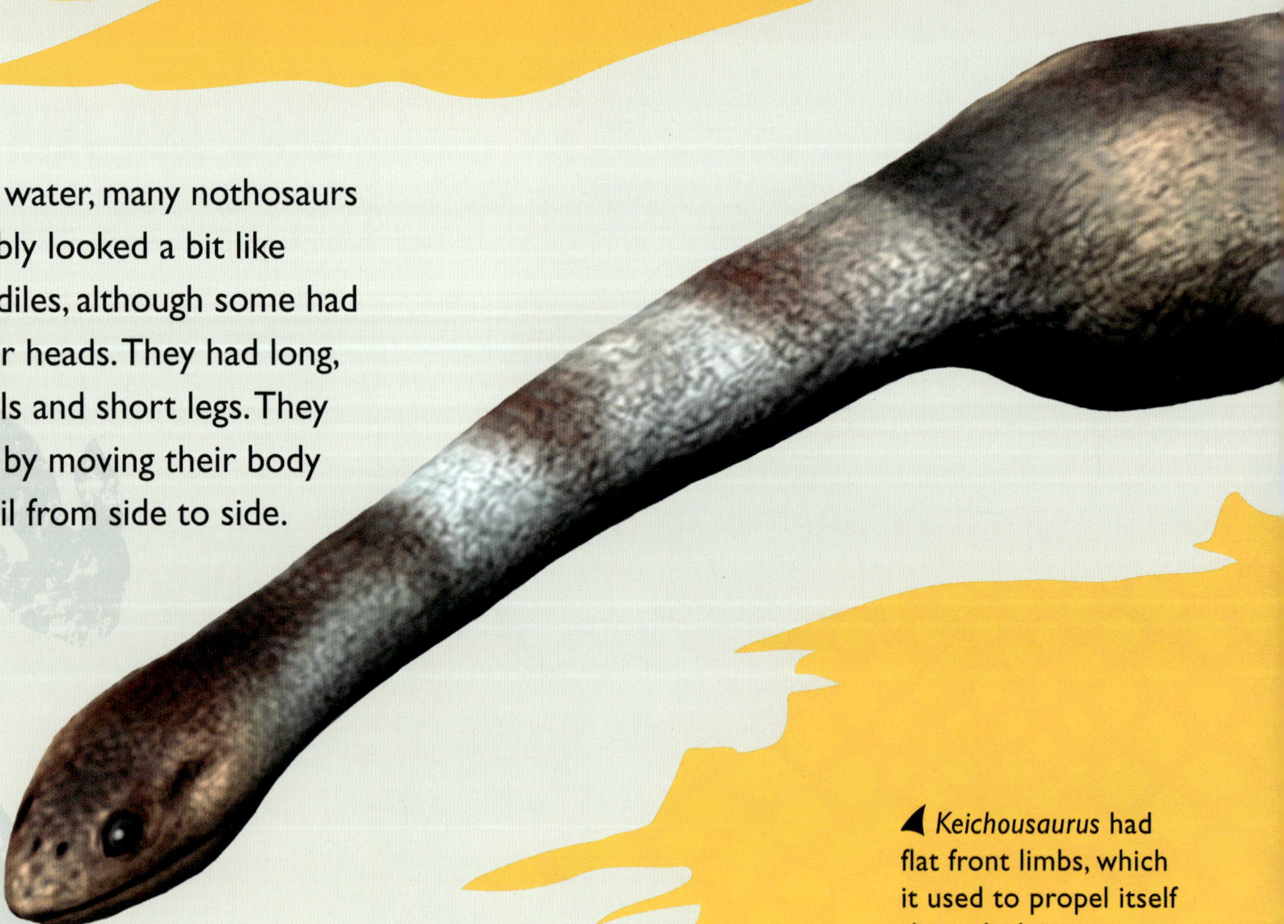

Keichousaurus had flat front limbs, which it used to propel itself through the water.

This *Lariosaurus* fossil shows some common features of the nothosaurs: a small head, long neck and five-toed feet.

Instead of flippers, the nothosaurs had webbed feet. Some species had claws on their feet, which suggests they could still walk on land. Like seals or sea lions today, the nothosaurs may have come to shore to bask in the sun. They probably laid their eggs on land too.

Most nothosaurs had long necks. Their flat heads were also elongated, but were quite small compared to the size of their bodies. Nothosaurs' long, sharp teeth pointed outwards slightly to help them catch and grip their prey, such as fish and squid.

The nothosaurs' long jaws were lined with rows of needle-sharp teeth.

SORTED:

NOTHOSAURUS

LIKE OTHER NOTHOSAURS, *NOTHOSAURUS* WAS SEMI-AQUATIC. IT PROBABLY LIVED ALONG THE COASTLINES OF THE TRIASSIC WORLD, SPENDING ITS LIFE BOTH IN AND OUT OF THE WATER.

QUICK FACTS

PERIOD:
Mid Triassic

LIVED IN:
Asia, Europe, North America

LENGTH:
13 feet (4 m)

WEIGHT:
up to 330 pounds (150 kg)

NECK AND HEAD

At the end of *Nothosaurus*'s long neck was a broad, flat head. This reptile may have been able to twist its head and neck sideways to catch passing prey as it moved underwater.

BODY AND TAIL

Nothosaurus had a long, slim body and a long tail. Some experts think this nothosaur may have had a fin on its tail, but they don't know for sure.

DINOMIGHTY!

Nothosaurus didn't only prey on small creatures such as shellfish. Fossils have been found with baby placodonts (see pages 6–7) inside them, and even another nothosaur–a small *Lariosaurus*!

TEETH

Nothosaurus had long, very sharp teeth. With its jaw closed, *Nothosaurus*'s teeth formed a kind of cage, which worked well for trapping slippery fish.

SWIMMING

Nothosaurus moved through the water by swishing its body from side to side. It also used its legs and web-toed feet to push itself forward.

BIG-EYED ICHTHYOSAURS

ICHTHYOSAURS ("FISH LIZARDS") WERE AMONG THE FIRST LARGE SEA REPTILES TO EMERGE. THEY INHABITED THE TRIASSIC SEAS ALONGSIDE THE PLACODONTS AND NOTHOSAURS. UNLIKE THOSE GROUPS, THE ICHTHYOSAURS WERE VERY SUCCESSFUL, SURVIVING UNTIL THE LATE CRETACEOUS PERIOD.

Shastasaurus may have been the largest ichthyosaur ever–perhaps as long as 69 feet (21 m).

Ichthyosaurs came in all different sizes. Some were only 3.3 feet (1 m) long, but the biggest may have been more than 65 feet (20 m). Most ichthyosaurs had a streamlined shape that allowed them to move smoothly and swiftly through the water. Smaller species may have been able to swim as fast as 25 miles (40 km) per hour.

Sunlight can't penetrate deep into the ocean, so ichthyosaurs had large eyes to help them see in the deep darkness. Their sensitive ears could also detect ripples in the water made by their fish prey.

Unlike the nothosaurs, ichthyosaurs were not adapted to life on land. They lived their whole lives in the water and even gave birth to live young underwater. Some experts think they may have behaved a bit like modern whales do, finding a sheltered place, such as a lagoon, to give birth.

▲ Ichthyosaurs, such as *Ichthyosaurus*, were shaped more like fish than other prehistoric reptiles, but they had arm and leg bones in their flippers, and bones in their tails, which fish don't have. That's how experts know they were reptiles.

► *Eurhinosaurus* had a very long snout, giving it the appearance of a swordfish.

SORTED:

SHONISAURUS

***SHONISAURUS* LIVED ONLY DURING THE LATE TRIASSIC PERIOD—A SHORT TIME COMPARED TO MANY OTHER PREHISTORIC CREATURES. BUT THANKS TO ALL THE FOSSILS THAT HAVE BEEN FOUND OF THIS ICHTHYOSAUR, IT IS ONE OF THE BEST-KNOWN SEA REPTILES.**

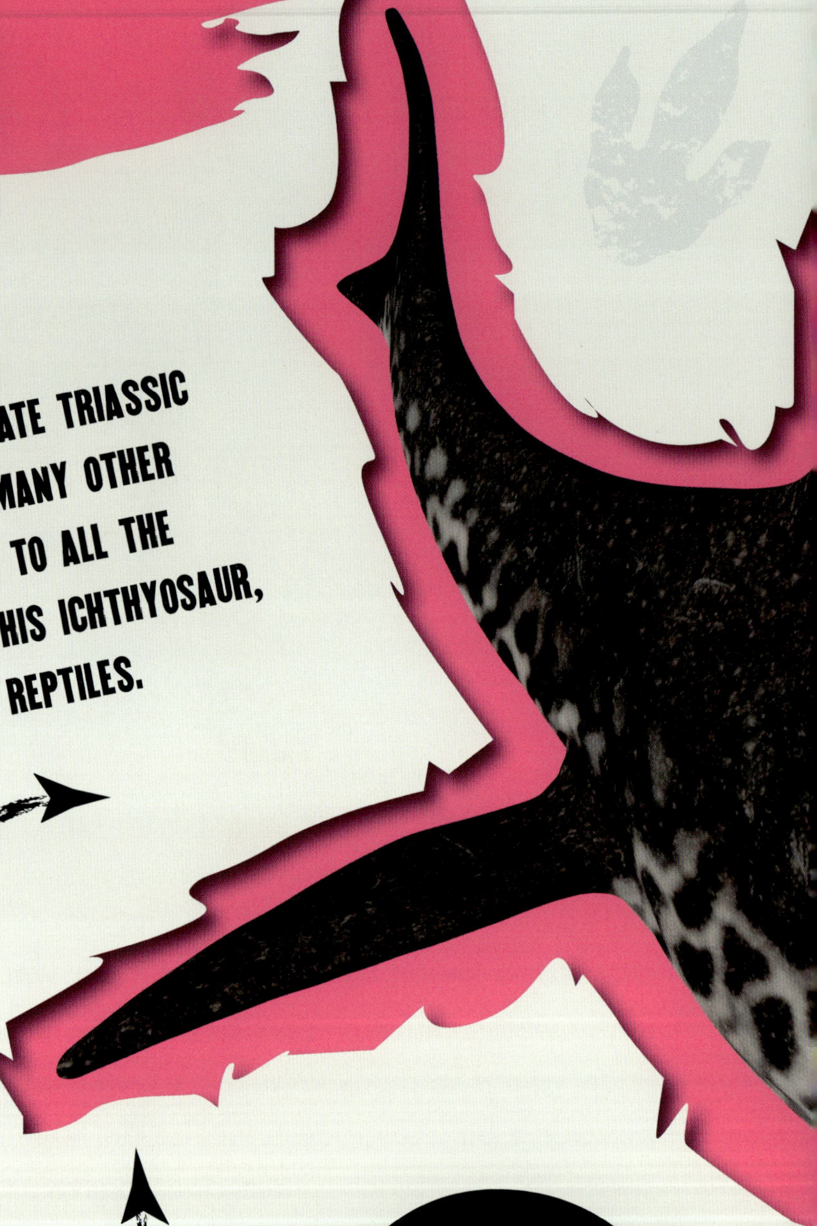

BODY SHAPE

Shonisaurus was shaped like a fish. Some paleontologists think it may have had a dorsal fin, although no evidence of this has ever been found. The fin may have been made of cartilage, which is softer than bone so is less likely to survive for millions of years.

FLIPPERS

Shonisaurus propelled itself through the water by moving its tail and body from side to side. It had four paddle-like flippers that were longer and narrower than those of many other members of the ichthyosaur family.

QUICK FACTS

PERIOD:
Late Triassic

LIVED IN:
North America

LENGTH:
16 feet (15 m)

WEIGHT:
up to 8,000 pounds (3,600 kg)

LARGE EYES

Like many ichthyosaurs, *Shonisaurus* had big eyes. This suggests that it may have spent time in deep waters, where sunlight could not reach.

DINOMIGHTY!

Shonisaurus's body was longer than a *Tyrannosaurus rex*'s!

LONG SNOUT

Shonisaurus had a very long snout. Unusually, adult *Shonisauruses* had no teeth at all. Young ones had some teeth at the front of the jaw, but these fell out before adulthood.

LONG-NECKED PLESIOSAURS

THE GROUP OF REPTILES KNOWN AS PLESIOSAURS EVOLVED IN THE LATE TRIASSIC PERIOD AND SURVIVED UNTIL THE END OF THE CRETACEOUS PERIOD. PLESIOSAURS SWAM IN THE SEAS ALL OVER THE WORLD, AND FOSSILS HAVE BEEN FOUND ON ALMOST EVERY CONTINENT.

Plesiosaurs had big bodies and small heads. In between was a long, slim, snake-like neck that was extremely flexible. In some species, such as *Muraenosaurus*, the neck could be 9.8 feet (3 m) long–half the creature's total length!

Styxosaurus may have been able to swim below shoals of fish, hiding its body in the deep, murky water and using its long neck to reach up and grab its prey.

Plesiosaurs had long, curved flippers instead of legs and feet like the nothosaurs (see pages 10–11). In some plesiosaurs, the flippers had several smaller joints, which made them very flexible. The flippers helped plesiosaurs swim swiftly through the water.

Plesiosaurus was one of the earliest plesiosaurs. It had a fairly wide body and a short tail.

Paleontologists think that plesiosaurs may have been bottom-feeders, which means they searched for food, such as clams, on the seabed. They probably also ate fish and squid. The plesiosaur would open its mouth and let fish flow in with the water. It would then close its jaws to create a cage to stop them escaping.

This skeleton of a *Plesiosaurus* shows its long flippers, which it moved up and down like a turtle does to move through the water.

SORTED:

ELASMOSAURUS

ELASMOSAURUS WAS ONE OF THE LARGEST PLESIOSAURS. IT WAS ALSO ONE OF THE LAST TO HAVE EXISTED, EMERGING IN THE LATE CRETACEOUS PERIOD AND DYING OUT IN THE MASS EXTINCTION EVENT AT THE END OF THAT ERA.

DINOMIGHTY!

Elasmosaurus's neck was so big and strong that experts think the reptile may have been able to lift it right out of the water! It could have stuck its head above the surface to breathe.

LONG NECK

Most modern reptiles have 5 to 10 vertebrae in their neck. Most plesiosaurs had 60, but *Elasmosaurus* outdid all of them! With 71 vertebrae, its flexible neck was extremely long–half of its total length.

QUICK FACTS

PERIOD:
Late Cretaceous

LIVED IN:
North America

LENGTH:
up to 50 feet (15 m)

WEIGHT:
6,000 pounds (2,700 kg)

FEEDING HABITS

Elasmosaurus probably ate sea creatures such as fish, squid, and ammonites. When feeding, it snaked its neck from side to side, searching for and catching prey. *Elasmosaurus* didn't have to waste energy chasing its food!

HEAD AND JAW

Elasmosaurus's eyes were close to the top of its head. This allowed it to see fish swimming above it and move swiftly to snap them up. In its jaw were rows of sharp teeth that clamped together to form a cage for its prey.

FLIPPERS

Elasmosaurus's four flippers were quite rigid. They acted like strong paddles to move its big body through the water.

FIERCE PLIOSAURS

PLIOSAURS WERE DESCENDED FROM THE SAME REPTILE ANCESTORS AS THE PLESIOSAURS. HOWEVER, THE TWO GROUPS EVOLVED TO HAVE QUITE DIFFERENT FEATURES.

The pliosaurs had huge heads compared to other groups of sea reptiles. When they were first discovered, the large skulls led people to think that the pliosaurs were larger than they actually were. Pliosaurs had nostrils on the top of their head, so they only had to break the surface of the water to breathe.

▲ *Liopleurodon* had a good sense of smell. It could smell the different scents of its prey under the water, the way a great white shark can.

Pliosaurs came in a range of sizes, from around 13 feet (4 m) up to about 40 feet (12 m), but whatever their size, they were fierce hunters! Most pliosaurs had strong jaws and large, serrated teeth. They may have hunted fish, sharks, other pliosaurs, and even dinosaurs.

Peloneustes had huge, strong jaws with cone-shaped teeth that were good for cracking the shells of shellfish.

Like the plesiosaurs, pliosaurs had two pairs of strong flippers to propel them through the water. One pair was at the front of the body, just below the neck. The other was positioned just above the tail.

Pliosaurs, such as the Jurassic *Simolestes*, had glands that got rid of salt. This meant that they could drink seawater without retaining too much salt in their bodies.

SORTED:

QUICK FACTS

PERIOD:
Early Cretaceous

LIVED IN:
Australia,
South America

LENGTH:
33 feet (10 m)

WEIGHT:
22,000 pounds (10,000 kg)

KRONOSAURUS

ONE OF THE MOST GIGANTIC PLIOSAURS, *KRONOSAURUS* WAS THE LORD OF ITS OCEAN KINGDOM. IT PREYED ON LARGE FISH, GIANT SQUID, AND MAYBE EVEN OTHER REPTILES, SUCH AS ICHTHYOSAURS.

APEX PREDATOR

Kronosaurus was an apex predator–so large that no other creature hunted it. It grew so big and powerful because it lived in the open ocean, where the water could support its great weight. It was a fearsome hunter, using its flippers to "fly" through the water.

HEAD AND BODY

Kronosaurus had a round body and a short neck. It is famous for its huge, long head–about 9 feet (2.7 m) of its 40-foot (12-m) length. Its tail was short and pointed. Its back flippers extended to about the same length as its tail. This was good for giving it quick bursts of speed.

TEETH

Kronosaurus's giant jaws were lined with 5-inch (12-cm) long teeth. Unlike most other pliosaurs, *Kronosaurus* didn't have serrated teeth. This suggests that it may have eaten smaller prey that it could swallow easily. It may also have taken larger prey and twisted its body violently to tear off chunks of flesh, the way a crocodile does.

DINOMIGHTY!

As if *Kronosaurus*'s enormous jaw wasn't scary enough, the first three upper teeth were elongated into terrifying fangs!

GIANT MOSASAURS

MOSASAURS WERE THE LAST MAIN GROUP OF SEA-LIVING REPTILES. THEY APPEARED AT THE START OF THE LATE CRETACEOUS PERIOD AND ALL DIED IN THE MASS EXTINCTION EVENT AT THE END OF IT. IN THAT TIME, THOUGH, THESE MONSTER REPTILES RULED THE OCEANS!

▲ *Tylosaurus* had more than 80 vertebrae in its tail, providing a powerful, flexible method of moving.

Mosasaurs came in many different sizes. Some species were only about 3.3 feet (1 m) long, but the biggest were giants of the deep, reaching up to 56 feet (17 m). They had a large, lizard-like body shape that was good for moving through water.

Most mosasaurs had long, broad tails, which they moved from side to side to power themselves along. Some later species may also have had flukes on the end of their tail, like a shark, to move them through the water.

Prognathodon had a large body and a huge skull.

With their large, hinged jaws, mosasaurs could grab prey and gulp it down whole, in a similar way to a snake. They also had blunt teeth that were useful for crushing creatures like shellfish. They feasted on fish, ammonites, and smaller mosasaurs.

Platecarpus had fewer teeth than other mosasaurs, probably because it had a short snout. Fossil teeth like these show that mosausaurs ate mostly fish, but may also have hunted ammonites.

SORTED:

MOSASAURUS

***MOSASAURUS* WAS A BIG OCEAN PREDATOR–BIGGER THAN MOST SHARKS TODAY. IT HUNTED MANY SEA CREATURES, INCLUDING THE GIANT, WELL-ARMORED SEA TURTLES THAT SHARED THE CRETACEOUS SEAS.**

QUICK FACTS

PERIOD:
Late Cretaceous

LIVED IN:
Africa, Asia, Europe, North America,
South America

LENGTH:
60 feet (18 m)

WEIGHT:
31,000 pounds (14,000 kg)

BIG BODY

Mosasaurus wasn't as huge as some other mosasaurs, but it was one of the heaviest-built. Because of its large body, it probably hunted slower-moving prey that couldn't dart away quickly. This may have included other sea reptiles and large fish such as sharks.

SWIMMING

Mosasaurus had small flippers with webs of skin between the bones. The flippers were too weak to have much effect when swimming. Instead, *Mosasaurus* probably moved its large body and long tail from side to side, like a shark, to move through the water.

DINOMIGHTY!

Mosasaurus had a double-hinged jaw. This would have allowed it to swallow large prey whole.

BREATHING

Like other reptiles, *Mosasaurus* breathed air through its nostrils. It probably spent most of its time near the surface of the water so it could poke its head up and breathe.

GLOSSARY

AMMONITE – a now-extinct sea creature with a spiral-patterned shell

ANCESTOR – someone or something from the same family, many generations earlier

ASTEROID – a large rock that forms in space and orbits the sun

CARAPACE – the hard upper shell of animals such as turtles and tortoises

CARTILAGE – a strong but flexible connective tissue in the body

DENTICLES – very thin, tooth-like structures positioned close together in the mouth that filter food underwater

DORSAL FIN – a triangular fin on the back of a fish or whale

FOSSIL – the shape of a plant or animal that has been preserved in rock for a very long time

GILLS – the organs on fish and some amphibians that allow them to breathe underwater

LAGOON – an area of salt water that is separated from the sea by a strip of land

MASS EXTINCTION – when many species stop existing completely

PALEONTOLOGIST – a scientist who studies dinosaurs and prehistoric life

PREDATOR – an animal that hunts other animals for food

SEMI-AQUATIC – describing animals that spend part of their life on land and part in water

SERRATED – having a jagged edge

SKULL – the bones that make up the head and face

SPECIES – a group of living things that are closely related and share similar features

STREAMLINED – describing a shape that is often narrow and pointed towards the front, in order to move easily through water or air

VERTEBRAE – the bones that make up the spine, or backbone (singular: vertebra)

FURTHER INFORMATION

BOOKS

Dictionary of Dinoaurs
By Matthew G. Baron, editor (Wide Eyed Editions, 2024)

Why? Dinosaurs
By Stephanie Warren Drimmer (National Geographic Kids, 2025)

WEBSITES

https://kids.nationalgeographic.com/animals/prehistoric
Check out more about all kinds of dinosaurs here.

www.nhm.ac.uk/discover/life-in-jurassic-oceans.html
Discover what life was like in the prehistoric seas.

ACTIVITY

Use the information in this book to design a new prehistoric sea reptile. Remember to include the features of whatever group you choose. Then give your reptile a name.

INDEX